Original title:
A Ring for Every Soul

Copyright © 2025 Creative Arts Management OÜ
All rights reserved.

Author: Jasper Montgomery
ISBN HARDBACK: 978-1-80586-186-7
ISBN PAPERBACK: 978-1-80586-658-9

Symbols of Eternal Unity

In a world full of bling,
The wobblers still swing.
We wear the bling with glee,
But can't find the key.

Tiny circles of fate,
With a hint of debate.
Some are big, some are small,
Yet we cherish them all.

The Roundness of Our Stories

Every tale goes around,
Like a merry-go-round.
We spin with laughter bright,
In the day and the night.

Those mismatched socks we wear,
With stories everywhere.
From fashion faux pas fun,
To baking too much bun.

Unity in the Dance of Life

Life's a dance, so they say,
With moves we can't betray.
We twirl and trip along,
All together, we're strong.

In mismatched shoes we prance,
Who knew we'd find romance?
Dancing in circles tight,
Till we giggle with delight.

Cycles of Love and Yearning

Love comes back like a boomerang,
With a wacky, joyful slang.
Though sometimes it may sting,
We'll always wear the ring.

In cycles, we will roam,
Finding our funny home.
With laughter in each chase,
We'll dance in endless grace.

Spinning Threads of Connection

In a world where yarns do tangle,
We knit our lives with a giggle.
With each stitch, a laugh we share,
Who knew life's a threadbare affair?

Sock-puppets dance, they take the stage,
Join hands in chaos, set the gauge.
We spin our tales, wobbly and bright,
Knitting bonds that feel just right.

The Infinity of Togetherness

Two peas in a pod, or so they say,
We bounce through life in a comical way.
Like infinite loops, we trip and twine,
In this wild circus, you're in line!

Juggling dreams, we drop a few,
Laughing at chaos, just me and you.
A rollercoaster ride, hold on tight,
Together we soar, in pure delight.

Unity's Sacred Loop

In circles we chase, around and around,
A merry-go-round with no solid ground.
We high-five the sky and tumble below,
Unity's dance has a wobbly flow.

Woven with jokes and playful tease,
We gather 'round, do as we please.
Stitching together, with laughter and grace,
In this zany world, we've found our place.

The Arc of Relationships

Swinging on arcs, we duck and dive,
In this wacky world, we're meant to thrive.
Like swing sets creaking in the breeze,
Our friendship's full of sweet, silly ease.

Pie in the face, who made that mess?
With chuckles and giggles, we bless the stress.
As seasons change and life moves fast,
We'll share our laughs, forever vast.

The Looped Reflection

In a world so round, we twirl and spin,
Collecting each laugh, through thick and thin.
We wear our jests like a fashionable hat,
In this quirky dance, where's the serious at?

Around and around, we chase our tails,
Trading our secrets, sharing our trails.
A joke in a circle, oh what a sight,
We'll roll on the floor, till we laugh out of sight.

Resonance of Shared Moments

We gather like bees, in a hive of delight,
Buzzing with stories, from morning to night.
Each moment a giggle, each glance a smile,
Twisting our tales, let's linger a while.

With punchlines like blossoms, we flourish and grow,
In the garden of laughter, our spirits in tow.
A nudge and a wink, as our stories unfold,
In this wacky world, we're a sight to behold.

Symphonies of Togetherness

We're a band of misfits, a motley crew,
Playing our tunes, so off-key but true.
With each little note, we create a scene,
Our laughs echo bright, like a giggling sheen.

We strum on our quirks, in harmony's light,
Dancing through chaos, oh what a sight!
No rehearsed symphony, just hearts in a whirl,
With humor our baton, we spin and unfurl.

The Embrace of Circles

In circles we gather, with snacks all around,
Cracking up jokes, till our bellies resound.
Round and around, let's toast with our cheer,
In this endless embrace, we've got nothing to fear.

We twirl on our chairs, like leaves in the air,
Tickling each other, with laughter to share.
A circle so cozy, you'll never be cold,
In this funny enclave, let the joys unfold.

Enchanted Loops

In a market of wishes, quite bizarre,
Sellers peddle loops from near and far.
One spun for laughter, another for cheer,
Each twist a promise, don't lose your ear!

Around the corner, a cat wore a band,
Claiming it granted a magical hand.
With every paw swipe, it jested and played,
In rings of delight, all troubles just frayed.

Heartfelt Circuits

Circuits of joy buzz under the sun,
Where techie hearts beat and circuits run.
Love's wired in laughter, sparks flying wide,
In each little loop, happy fools take pride.

Dates planned in loops, oh what a blend,
One guy wore a necklace, it stuck to his friend.
With laughter and circuits, they danced to the sound,
In deep tangled garlands, their love newly found.

Legacy of the Circle

Grandma's one-liners were shaped like a ring,
Her wisdom in spirals, oh what a fling!
With each little chuckle, a legacy shared,
In circles of humor, she always dared!

Her garden's a riot, with gnomes all around,
Each one holds a story, in laughter they're bound.
In heirlooms so quirky, her spirit will twirl,
A legacy cherished in each jolly swirl.

Entwined Destinies

Two socks in the dryer, a curious fate,
Whirling in circles, oh isn't it great?
Each twist and each turn, a dance odd yet fun,
In laundry's embrace, two souls become one!

At parties we gather, our quirks intertwined,
With jokes that loop back, they echo, aligned.
Destinies tangled in laughter's sweet jest,
In circles we thrive, oh what a fest!

The Language of Loops

In circles we go, like wheels on a bus,
Chasing our tails, without any fuss.
Each loop that we make, a giggle or two,
Who knew such a spiral could cause this hullabaloo?

Round and around, we spin in delight,
Tangled in laughter, in day and in night.
Our chatter like loops, a curious dance,
With every bounce back, we give it a chance.

In loops we confide, our secrets held tight,
Not knowing the end, just savoring the flight.
With every little twist, more joy we unfold,
Playing along as the stories are told.

Whirligigs of Shared Dreams

Spin me a tale, a whirligig bright,
A dance of our dreams, in the warm moonlight.
Round we will go, with giggles galore,
Who knew sharing dreams could open a door?

In circles we chase, oh what a delight,
Puffing like popcorn, oh what a sight!
With each little twirl, our worries take wing,
Together we laugh at the joy that we bring.

On this merry-go-round, life's ups and downs,
We twist and we shout, we wear silly crowns.
Round and again, let's keep spinning tight,
In whirlwinds of joy, everything feels right.

The Spiral of Companionship

A spiral of giggles, we twirl in a rush,
Each move forward brings a jubilant hush.
With arms intertwined, we dance through the day,
In this zigzag of friendship, come what may.

Round we navigate, in our silly parade,
With snorts and with chuckles, our worries allayed.
Each twist of our fate, a hearty embrace,
In the loop of companionship, we find our place.

Like a rollercoaster ride, so wild and so true,
We whirl and we waltz, just me and you.
In laughter we spiral, through thick and through thin,
Together we shine, as we spin and we grin.

Melodies of Entwined Souls

In harmonies sweet, our laughter takes flight,
Two souls like a duet, ringing out bright.
With each silly note, we craft a bizarre tune,
Our melodies dancing, a joyous monsoon.

Spinning together, we write our own song,
In this playful tune, we both sing along.
With every twist, we find more to delight,
A perfect duet, in the soft moonlight.

Entwined in our rhythms, we bounce to the beat,
Creating a symphony, playful and sweet.
Two souls waltzing round, in laughter's embrace,
Together we twirl, with sheer glee on our face.

Compass of Hearts

In a land of lost socks, my heart took flight,
It spun around like a kite in the night.
With a compass so crooked, I followed the game,
Chasing odd treasures, oh, what a shame!

Through puddles and giggles, I navigated well,
My map was a doodle, with stories to tell.
Following laughter, I turned left and right,
Found a cupcake shop, what a wonderful sight!

The Rhythm of Circles

I danced in the kitchen, I tripped on a spoon,
Spinning in circles, I hummed a tune.
The dog joined the party, he wagged and he barked,
With each little twirl, our joy simply sparked!

Rotating our worries, we laughed like mad,
Each wobble a mishap, yet we never were sad.
In this circus of chaos, I found my best mate,
We circled the island, oh goodness, so great!

Chains of Sentiment

With links made of laughter, we clinked and we clanked,
Our hearts all connected, though we often pranked.
We wore silly beads, and we danced in the rain,
Each giggle's a bond that needs no explain!

We forged goofy chains, made from tales of delight,
Fell over our dreams, like dogs in a fight.
Tangled together in a whirl of pure fun,
In this chain of madness, we let our hearts run!

The Confluence of Journeys

On paths intertwined, we stumbled and slid,
With backpacks of nonsense, we laughed like we did.
A map full of hiccups, we trekked on with flair,
Through gardens of giggles, oh, the views we would share!

At the junction of jests, we painted the sky,
With colors of jokes that made grumpy souls fly.
In this mess of adventures, our hearts beat as one,
Each turn was a joke, oh, the fun never done!

Threads of Forever

In a world of tangled strings,
We laugh and dance, oh how it sings!
A loop of joy that never bends,
Each knot we tie, another friend.

With stickers stuck and laughter loud,
We bind our hearts, we form a crowd.
A twist of fate, a silly prank,
Together, we'll fill up the tank!

When threads get loose and lose the way,
We patch it up, come what may.
With bubbles blown and jokes to share,
Our friendship's spark is always there.

So here's to bonds that brightly shine,
In every twist, your hand in mine.
We'll weave a tale, just don't forget,
Our laughter is the best preset!

Tokens of Bond and Trust

In cupboards filled with shiny things,
We trade our snacks like grand kings.
With candy wrappers, we declare,
This token's yours; I do not care!

A lack of sense in every pact,
We share our socks, that's a fact!
You take my left, I'll have the right,
Together we'll be quite a sight!

The coins we toss in fountains deep,
Are wishes made, oh what a leap!
But if you lose, don't pout or fret,
We'll count our treasures, no regret.

So gather round and raise a cheer,
For silly tokens, far and near.
In every giggle, every jest,
Our bonds are truly the very best!

Circular Promises

A donut shared, oh what delight,
We seal our vows with every bite.
With sprinkles bright and chocolate deep,
These circular promises we keep.

A wheel of cheese, oh let's indulge,
In cheesy jokes, we never bulge.
Round and round like merry-go,
Our laughter flows, it's quite the show.

For every loop, a silly tale,
We ride the waves, we will not pale.
A circle drawn in crayon bright,
Our doodled dreams take off in flight!

So here's to circles, never square,
With hugs and laughs we'd always share.
Round and round our fun will roll,
In every spiral, we find our soul!

Whispers of Eternal Union

In chocolate whispers, secrets blend,
With fudgy love, we always mend.
A scoop of fun, a sprinkle here,
Together we'll spread silly cheer.

A playful breeze that swirls around,
In giggles soft, our joy is found.
We whisper wishes in the night,
And dance around, oh what a sight!

With every secret, bonds will grow,
In whispered tales, we steal the show.
A painted heart on sidewalk bright,
We leave our mark with sheer delight.

So here's to whispers, sweet and sly,
With laughter shared, we touch the sky.
In every chuckle, joy we summon,
In this grand play, our hearts are one!

Mystic Bonds

In a world where cuffs stray,
And socks play hide and seek,
A bracelet calls my name,
While my cat gives a squeak.

To promise forever, they say,
But forgot the size, you see,
A banquet of mismatched gems,
Did the dog plan this spree?

Each gem tells a tale, so wild,
Of grandma's secret stash,
Or the time my shoe had fled,
And left me with a crash.

In cosmic jest, we dance along,
With laughter as our guide,
For every quirk, a bond is strong,
In chaos, love won't hide.

Bound in the Loop

Came a twist that caught me well,
A circle made of cheese,
We laughed until we hit the floor,
In our silly, endless tease.

Two rubber bands, all stretched and worn,
A promise to each mate,
Yet through mishaps and all the scorn,
We find our goofy fate.

The yarn gets tangled with delight,
Like verses in a song,
And while we aim for all that's right,
We stumble all along.

With each quirky bond we create,
We seal a laugh or two,
In jolly loops, we celebrate,
With heartstrings wrapped in glue.

Threads of Intertwined Fates

In the weft and weave of life,
Our paths get crossed each day,
A rogue thread in the bustling loom,
Idiosyncratic play.

From mismatched shoes to cheesy grins,
Each stitch a tale to tell,
With laughter bent around our kin,
Who knew oddity spells?

Tangled hair and knotted dreams,
Like spaghetti in a pot,
Yet in those twists, affection beams,
In every jumbled knot.

So here's to threads that bind us tight,
In whimsies we find grace,
For in the crazy, fun, and light,
We embrace our quirky space.

Orbiting Affection

Around we spin in playful glee,
With wobbling hearts that dance,
Like planets lost in destiny,
We stumble through romance.

Our hugs are comets, bright and bold,
With trails that leave a mark,
While jellybeans and stories told,
Create our timeless arc.

In the cosmos of our laughter,
We'll find a way to soar,
Making joy our ever-after,
In hugs and sticky lore.

As satellites of goofy fun,
We travel, side by side,
In orbit's twist, we're never done,
For love's our crazy ride.

Symbols of Devotion

A circle so round, it fits like a glove,
Ties us together, just like a dove.
With silver and gold, we mark our days,
In laughter and love, we dance and play.

In thrift stores we search for the perfect find,
A charm for each moment, one of a kind.
With each little gift, our hearts intertwine,
Wearing socks with our rings, oh how divine!

With bling on our fingers, we strut with glee,
Although some think we wear it to tease.
For loyalty's shiny, sometimes it slips,
As long as it sparkles, we'll still take the trips.

So here's to the tokens, both comical and clear,
In our wacky collection, we hold them dear.
For what's a bit laughter, but love's finest thread?
With rings on our fingers, we'll dance 'til we're dead!

Celestial Embrace

The stars in the sky, in circles they twirl,
Like kiddies in love, in a dizzying whirl.
They spin and they shine, with winks and a grin,
Making wishes come true; let the fun begin!

There's Jupiter's charm and Saturn's tight hug,
We'll throw in a comet for a little more snug.
With each cosmic circle, we giggle and gawk,
Who knew in the heavens, we all could talk?

We argue with asteroids over dessert,
While Venus throws shade, we just laugh and flirt.
Fairy tales woven on celestial beams,
Our goofy embrace is more than it seems.

So skydive through laughter in cosmic delight,
With rings spanning galaxies, oh what a sight!
In the embrace of the cosmos, we find our joy,
Rings left behind are the stars we'll deploy!

Legacy of Connected Souls

In friendship we gather, our laughter rings true,
With each silly prank, it's a bond we renew.
Like bracelets of yarn that we craft with our hands,
In this quirky legacy, everybody stands.

With socks that don't match and hairdos askew,
We proclaim our unity, colorful crew!
A legacy made of inside jokes and cheer,
Connected by quirks, we have nothing to fear.

As we stack up our treasures, odd memories swirl,
From late-night confessions to dancing a twirl.
Through laughter and chaos, we form our pact,
Creating a legacy, that's fun and intact!

So here's to the ring of our goofy delight,
In moments together, we shine ever bright.
A connected family, through thick and through thin,
With a legacy crafted, let the fun begin!

Allure of the Circular Path

Around and around, on this merry-go-round,
With giggles and wiggles, we're joyfully bound.
The paths that we take make us laugh till we weep,
In circles of fun, our moments we keep.

With donuts and hula hoops, we spin with glee,
Who knew that a circle could set our hearts free?
In this wacky journey, we take little detours,
Through silly mishaps, our humor endures.

Like children on swings, flying high in the air,
We're chasing our dreams, without any care.
On this circular path, we hold hands so tight,
With laughter as fuel, oh what a delight!

So gather your friends, let's chase after fate,
In a circle of joy, we'll never be late.
For the allure of this journey, it's clear in our minds,
Circles of laughter and fun are what binds!

Bound by a Whisper

A circle of laughter, what a delight,
Friends join in giggles, day turns to night.
Each one's a puzzle, a quirky part,
Linking our tales like a wild work of art.

A chain of oddball, we dance in sync,
At the coffee shop, we lose all our ink.
Marking our stories with sips and some sweets,
A jumbled fraternity of charming retreats.

In the car, we bicker, no means to an end,
Jokes fly like missiles, we can't help but send.
A chorus of laughter, that's how we roll,
With a wacky connection, we all feel whole.

So here's to the moments, both silly and free,
Life's hilarious symphony, just you wait and see.
In our own little circle, we twirl and we spin,
Together, forever, let the good times begin!

Celestial Links

Stars in the sky, they twinkle and shout,
A cosmic connection, no shadow of doubt.
Every blip tells a tale, absurd and bright,
Linking us all in a glittery flight.

Planets align like a fancy parade,
Orbiting friendship, no need to be staid.
With giggles and snorts, we bounce through the night,
Creating a nebula of pure delight.

Asteroids tumble, like us on the floor,
Colliding with laughter, we giggle for more.
In this vast universe, we're a band so bold,
Crafting our stories, with humor retold.

So raise up your glasses, let's toast to the skies,
To our cosmic jests and our interstellar ties.
Together we sparkle, like stars in the sea,
In a galaxy of fun, just you and me!

The Cycle of Togetherness

Life spins in circles, a merry-go-round,
We hop on with laughter, joy knows no bounds.
Round and around, we chase our own tails,
In this carousel ride, humor prevails.

From sunrise to sunset, hand in hand we sway,
With quirks and with giggles, we brighten the day.
Every twist and turn is a comical drawer,
Unlocking our secrets and so much more.

Twisting and turning, we break into grins,
Sharing our fumbles, where the fun always wins.
As each giddy spin brings a chuckle or two,
In this dance of delight, it's just me and you.

So laugh with abandon, let your worries go,
In the cycle of friendship, we steal the show.
Round and around, with our hearts intertwined,
In the laughter we cherish, our spirits aligned!

Infinity's Caress

Endless giggles wrap us like a warm hug,
In a playful embrace, we snuggle and shrug.
Time may keep ticking, but we stay aglow,
In our own little world where the funny seeds grow.

We bounce like rubber, through moments of cheer,
Rolling in laughter, we've nothing to fear.
Infinite antics that spiral in place,
Together our tapestry finds its own grace.

Jokes come in waves, they crash and they swell,
Collect them like seashells, take turns to tell.
With each nutty story, we tally and trace,
In this timeless circle, we find our own space.

So revel in the mayhem, let laughter flow free,
In our infinity, just you and me.
With quirks intertwined, and a smile that won't lie,
We'll ride this wild journey, as life passes by!

Molding Memories in Metal

In a shop where dreams are formed,
Laughter fills the air, quite warmed.
Getting sizes, oh what a chore,
Who knew fingers could be such a bore?

He said, "This one is snug, not quite right!"
She laughed and said, "Next time, use might!"
Upon this metal, our quirks we twist,
Caught giggling in a golden mist.

A wink here, a nudge there, oh how we jest,
Each ring a tale, a humorous quest.
Fingers pointing, each stone a joke,
Who wears it better? A playful poke!

Through blunders and mishaps, we create,
Jewels of joy, never to hesitate.
In laughter's embrace, our bond we hold,
In shiny circles, our stories unfold.

Circles of Kinship

Round and round, our stories spin,
With each twist, more mischief begins.
A tiny ring, but oh, such a tale,
It slipped off! Quick! One must prevail!

Family ties wrapped in shiny gold,
Circled together, never too old.
Who gets the biggest? The fiercest debate,
While the cat swipes at, isn't life great?

"More bling is better!" someone will chime,
As we bicker and laugh, oh so sublime.
Matching bands for our coats, we jest,
No one wears a ring without a quest!

These circles of joy, so full of glee,
Marking occasions like a jubilee.
Wearing our humor like jewels on display,
In this kinship, we find our way.

Harmonies of the Bond

Singing in circles, our voices blend,
Every ring tells what we defend.
From wobbly notes to perfect pitch,
Antics that make each other twitch!

Dancing and twirling, the rings will sway,
"Watch this move!" we shout and play.
In harmony, we craft our tune,
With a side of giggles, from sun to moon!

A melody shared, a silly glance,
Jewels and laughter in a joyful dance.
When one slips, we all will chuckle,
A waltz in diamonds, gold, and buckle!

Bonding over pranks, oh what a ride,
With rings to show, we take great pride.
In this cacophony of laughter bold,
Our interconnectedness is pure gold.

Everlasting Echoes

Whispers of secrets, laughter does flow,
Each echo carries stories we know.
Like metals that shimmer, our bonds ignite,
In timeless tales, bringing delight!

A clink of a ring, who's the loudest here?
With jokes and jests, we hold so dear.
Every clash a memory set to roam,
In joyful jingles, we find our home!

Circling the stories, our voices collide,
The joy of connection we never hide.
With echoes that linger, our laughter will tell,
What each little ring knows oh so well!

In this funny tale, echoes run deep,
In laughter and love, forever we leap.
With every twist, our stories will wave,
Across the ages, sweet memories we save.

The Circle that Binds Us

In a kingdom full of bling,
The squirrels all take wing.
With nuts stacked high, they buy and swap,
Each shining piece makes them hop!

One tiny acorn blurted out,
"I'm the king, without a doubt!"
But another said with gleeful cheer,
"This circle's best when friends are near!"

Round and round they danced with glee,
While wearing rings of shiny brie.
The laughter echoed through the land,
As silly secrets slipped from hand.

They craft new bands from roots and twine,
A ring's just cute, but friends define.
With every circle, there's a jest,
In friendship's ring, we find our best!

In Search of Sacred Unions

Two cats met on a fence one day,
"Let's form a club, what do you say?"
They searched for jewels beneath the stars,
But ended up with shiny cars!

A dog joined in, quite proud and spry,
"I'll fetch the goods, just watch me fly!"
But with each prize, he'd chase his tail,
And the quest turned into quite a tale.

With ties of threads and playful chants,
They tried to seal their silly pants.
Yet every time they made a vow,
A gust of wind would shout, "Not now!"

So under moonlight, they did conspire,
To trade the rings for socks of fire!
In laughter's glow, they found their prize,
True bonds can't hide, and that's no surprise!

Spirals of Heartfelt Vows

A chicken danced while wearing gold,
Said, "With this charm, I'll never grow old!"
But when it slipped, oh what a mess,
The rooster quacked, "My dear, confess!"

As spirals formed around the coop,
They twirled in synchrony, what a troupe!
With every leap, the vows unwound,
In feathers bright, pure joy they found.

A sock puppet joined to play a role,
Claiming it knew the secret goal.
Yet every time they reached the peak,
The jokes would fly, the giggles sneak!

So on they swirled, both loud and proud,
Spinning tales beneath the cloud.
For in their spirals, vows took flight,
Heartfelt humor made the night bright!

Links of Fate and Desire

In a bakery sweet with frosted rings,
A cat declared, "I love these things!"
But the dog sneezed, and what a blast,
The links of fate flew all too fast!

They chased the pastries down the street,
Each roll and croissant a tasty treat.
With laughter linking paw and claw,
Their friendship grew, a wondrous law.

A bird above cawed loud with glee,
"What's better than sweets and company?"
Each stolen crumb a testament,
To bonds of laughter, never spent.

So in their feast, desires twirled,
In sugary dreams, their joy unfurled.
With links of fate and food to share,
In every bite, their hearts laid bare!

The Circular Embrace

In a crowd of giggles and grins,
Everyone's dancing, it's how life begins.
Give me your hand, let's spin around,
We'll form a circle without making a sound.

With mismatched socks and silly hats,
We twist and twirl, just like acrobats.
A wobble here, a stumble there,
Laughter erupts, filling the air.

As the music plays, we move as one,
This silly dance has just begun.
Joyful chaos, a riot of cheer,
With every spin, we draw each other near.

So grab a friend, no time to waste,
Let's spin together with silly haste.
In this round embrace, we find our way,
Laughter's the glue that will always stay.

Unity Crafted in Silver

Four friends sat round, a table of fun,
Each sharing dreams beneath the sun.
With cups of coffee and cupcakes galore,
They plotted a scheme to create something more.

A band of rings, bright and shiny,
Each one winks, not a bit whiny.
Crafted with laughter, each twist and turn,
They giggled and cheered, for what they yearn.

One ring says 'Giggle', the other 'Goof',
Together they surely form a cartoon roof.
United in jest, no room for frowns,
The world's but a stage for their silly crowns.

So here's to the friends, the merry design,
Each sparkly piece, a bond that'll shine.
In silver and fun, they'll dance through the night,
Crafting memories that will twinkle bright.

The Magician's Circle

A magician stands in a hat so tall,
With a wand to wave that's ready to call.
"Watch closely now, for the trick is grand!"
He whispers secrets, waving his hand.

Out pops a rabbit, then a chicken struts,
Confetti showers, and laughter erupts!
"Did you see that? A circle of cheer!
Magic is real when friends are near!"

With a flick and a flurry, the crowd is amazed,
In this swirling circus, they're all crazed.
Each trick more funny than the last one spun,
Living the magic, just having fun!

With every laugh, the circle grows tight,
In this whimsical world, all feel just right.
So let's raise a toast to the magic we share,
For in this funny circle, there's always a flare.

Constellations of Connection

Under the stars, a cosmic delight,
Friends gather 'round, hearts shining bright.
Each twinkling light tells a tale so bold,
Of laughter and joy, worth more than gold.

"Look there!" one calls, "That star's like my shoe!
It's lost and it's silly, just like our crew!"
They point to the heavens, each joke takes flight,
Creating constellations that burst with delight.

The sky's their canvas, each story's a spark,
Painting the night with laughter after dark.
In this comedy show, they find their place,
Bound by the joy, the smiles, and grace.

So look up and laugh, let your heart sing,
For each star's a friend—yes, that's the thing!
With connections so bright, the night's a delight,
In their constellation of fun, all feels just right.

A Circle of Kindred Spirits

In a land where laughter roams,
We wear our charms like fancy gnomes.
With rings of onion and twisty ties,
Our unity sparkles, oh how it flies!

We gather 'round with goofy grins,
Exchanging tales of our silly sins.
A loop, a link, a jest or two,
Our bonds are strong, and so much askew!

With each new trinket, a story unfolds,
Of dancing penguins and treasure of gold.
Like playful cats that pounce and twirl,
We spin through life, watch laughter unfurl!

So here's to us, the merry crew,
Wearing thick bands of jello, who knew?
In a circle that sparkles and circles about,
Our kindred spirits will never pout!

Unity Beyond Borders

Across the globe, we raise our cheers,
With funky hats and even funky beards.
From tacos to tea, we share our plate,
Our world a loop, and oh, how great!

Balloons and flags, we wave in bliss,
With every mishap, there's laughter and hiss.
We dance the tango while eating cake,
In a kaleidoscope swirl, there's no mistake!

When an ostrich walks in, our jaws drop low,
With a laugh that erupts, the fun starts to flow.
United we stand, with puny delight,
Funny hats on heads, what a sight!

So here's to our quirks, to what makes us, us,
From beaches to mountains, we gather with trust.
Together we shine, like colors so bright,
In our melting pot, we take flight!

The Halo of Togetherness

A halo of laughter, we wear on our heads,
With wiggly wigs and twinkling threads.
Spin around, let the giggles ignite,
As we play dress-up and wear our delight!

With silly voices and chicken dance flair,
Our friendships bloom like flowers in air.
From jogging to waltzing, we'll joyfully sway,
Under the moonlight, come what may!

A pet goldfish joins, with a snappy little grin,
We toss him a snack and let the fun begin.
With every joke, our spirits nearly soar,
In this circle of friends, we always want more!

So here's to the giggles and crumbs on the floor,
To cheesy puns and moments we adore.
A halo of joy, we wear ever bright,
With hearts full of laughter, we take flight!

Embracing the Loop

In the twist of fate, we find our place,
With rubber bands stretching, oh what a race!
From yo-yos to hula hoops, round and round,
Life is a joke with giggles unbound!

We set off on journeys with maps made of candy,
Sailing on donuts, isn't that dandy?
Through loops and curls, our adventures sway,
Creating tales that brighten the day!

Hot air balloons, oh what a sight,
Floating on giggles, hearts feeling light.
With laughter as fuel, we twist and we twirl,
In this grand loop, we laugh and we whirl!

So gather your friends, let the fun now commence,
In a circle of laughter, we all make sense.
Round and round in our silly parade,
Embracing the loop, our joy won't fade!

Dimensions of Trust

In a universe quite absurd,
Where trust is rarely heard,
A handshake turns to slapstick,
As secrets make us feel so thick.

In a world of tangled strings,
Where laughter dances and sings,
We trade our quirks like gems so bright,
Making depth from sheer delight.

Trust is a wobbly tower,
That sometimes gives you power,
But knock it once, it starts to sway,
And sends your secrets on their way.

Yet through the giggles and the fuss,
We find our joy in silly trust,
For in this dance of oddy grace,
Every laugh's a warm embrace.

The Bond of Unseen Paths

We wander down these hidden trails,
Where friendship's wind lifts our sails,
With every bump we stop and laugh,
The universe shows its funny half.

In the crowd we make our way,
Waving to strangers like it's play,
The bonds we share are mischief spun,
With each new face, our hearts weigh tons.

Life's a game of hide and seek,
Where even silence starts to speak,
Through giggles shared behind a bush,
We find our kin in movement's hush.

Unseen paths that twist and wind,
Are just the routes we choose to find,
As we tumble through the laughs and sighs,
Each bond formed, a sweet surprise.

Eternal Whirls of Affection

In the whirlwind of our sway,
Affection spins in wild ballet,
With every twirl, a giggle slips,
As we dance to our friendship's quips.

Round and round in clockwise craze,
Life's a dizzy set ablaze,
With every embrace, a tickle thrown,
In this circus, we've brightly grown.

Love's a rollercoaster ride,
Where silly faces and jokes abide,
We hold on tight, through ups and downs,
Wearing laughter as our crowns.

In this swirl of jester's glee,
We find eternity, you and me,
In every whirl, we sway and spin,
Eternally laughing, the joy within.

Life's Golden Circumference

Life rolls round like a golden ball,
Rich with laughter, we stand tall,
With every turn, a funny face,
Our quirks, a merry, warm embrace.

Around the circle we chase our dreams,
In a world where nothing seems,
To stay straight—oh what a task!
We shuffle shoes and watch them bask.

With each trip and every tumble,
We find joy in the silly jumble,
Life's golden ring is worn with flair,
Where smiles are traded, everywhere.

And as we spin through joy and fuss,
Together in this golden bus,
We share the quirks and funny doubts,
In life's circumference, love shouts.

Time's Emblem of Inclusion

In a shop with gems so bright,
Everyone wants a shiny sight.
Some choose gold, others pick blue,
But what's a ring with no fondue?

The men wear bands that fit just right,
While girls stack rings with all their might.
Each gem a laugh, each glint a tease,
Just don't ask them how to freeze!

Grandma's in the corner with flair,
Says a ring can't match her pet hair.
She shows off one shaped like a fish,
Oh, darling, now that's a weird wish!

With every jest, they spin and dance,
Adorning fingers in a trance.
For every laugh, there's one more twist,
To finger bling, they can't resist!

The Roundabout of Affection

In a town where hearts collide,
Every ring is quite the ride.
Some are squares, some are rhombus,
But round's the ring with all the fun us!

Cupid's shop has choices galore,
Each ring's a wink, a playful chore.
Some folks choose hearts, big and bold,
While others like their bling on hold.

A squirrel slid by with diamond flair,
Asked for one that matched his hair.
The townsfolk giggle, shrug, and grin,
Who knew a rodent could so win?

On every hand, there's laughs to glean,
As rings and jokes become a scene.
In the roundabout, affection spins,
With every jest, a smile begins!

Chains of Serenity

In the breezy park, we play for keeps,
Where every chain's a laughter steep.
Some link fingers with such great pride,
While others just let wishes slide.

A cat wearing gold made quite the fuss,
Demanded a chain that came with a bus.
The bird looked on, with beady eyes,
Said a necklace attracts fat flies!

Grandpa laughs with a charm so grand,
Declares it brings luck like a band.
Yet, his linked gems bounce and sway,
As he trips over them in play.

Each connection tells a tale so bright,
With every link, there's pure delight.
In chains of giggles, we all bask,
Serenity's hidden in every task!

Segments of Serenity

Oh, the segments of life stack high,
In a bracelet that makes laughter fly.
Each piece a puzzle, full of cheer,
But don't ask why we're all here!

A segment's added for the fun,
It shines like gold under the sun.
Mix and match, a wild display,
But does it fit? We'll never say!

A child walks by with a tiny bell,
Clinks and clanks, oh what a swell.
'Is that a ring?' the elder exclaims,
'It's just her toy,' but oh the games!

Yet with each click, a giggle grows,
In segments of joy, it freely flows.
Life's a mix of awkward glee,
In a playful ring, can't you see?

Harmonies Bound by Circular Grace

In a town where laughter swells,
The dog wore pearls, and the cat tells tales.
A lady danced in neon shoes,
While frogs croaked out the evening news.

Kids in circles with sticky hands,
Made candy rings from licorice strands.
They crowned each other, king and queen,
In this wacky world, so sweet and keen.

With hoops of joy and giggles loud,
They formed a smiling, swirling crowd.
Each twirl and twist, a show of grace,
In this circle-dance, they found their place.

So here's to the ties that overlap,
With hearts like dough, we stretch and clap.
In rings of glee, we boldly fall,
Creating magic that binds us all.

Connexions Woven in Gold

A squirrel in shades, sunglasses on,
Sipped lemonade on the front lawn.
With a donut ring upon its tail,
It danced around like a happy whale.

The birds all strutted with diamond flair,
Perched on branches without a care.
While bees debated the best ring tone,
Buzzing songs that made them feel at home.

Frogs wore hats and sipped from cups,
While chasing down some bouncing pups.
In funny circles, they shared the jest,
Creating bonds that felt the best.

So raise a glass to sparkly threads,
And silly ties that bind our heads.
In this wild world of gold and song,
Together's where we all belong!

Frozen Moments in Endless Loops

A hamster with a hula hoop,
Commanded a grand, indoor troop.
They practiced moves with stellar flair,
While birds cheered on from the air.

Each loop they made a joyful shout,
As squirrels jumped and rolled about.
With twirling tails like cotton candy,
The laughter spread, it felt so dandy.

The rhythm kept them on their toes,
With furry jackets and silly clothes.
They chanted tunes from days of yore,
In circle fun, always wanting more.

So here's to moments, merry and bright,
In endless loops of pure delight.
Let's freeze these laughs in joyful frames,
In circles where we play the games!

The Joining of Heartstrings

A cat with yarn and a mouse so bold,
Joined together in a tale retold.
They spun around in dizzying circles,
Creating chaos, like playful turtles.

In every twist, a giggle or two,
As frogs played finders with a rabbit crew.
With strings of laughter, they stitched their fate,
In this merry dance, they just can't wait.

The dance was loud, each step a blast,
With every bounce, they floated past.
In jest and cheer, they sang their song,
In circles, they grew, the love grew strong.

So join the fun, swing wide and free,
With joyful ties, just come and see.
In heartstrings weaving, moments delight,
We find our joy, our spirits light.

Encircled Hearts

In a circle we find our cheer,
A pie chart of love, oh so clear.
With cookies galore and laughs by the door,
Each bite a reminder of what we hold dear.

Round like a hula, we twirl and spin,
Catching the giggles, that's how we win.
Forget all the squares, they just bring us gloom,
In these circles of joy, there's always more room.

Our lives all entwined, like spaghetti on plates,
With sauce made of laughter and fun on the fates.
We twine and we bend, just like a good vine,
In this wacky circus, we're truly divine.

So let's wear our rings, made of silly string,
A fashion statement, let's see what it brings.
With every spin, let's ignite the delight,
In our funny circle, everything feels right.

Infinite Connections

We connect like Wi-Fi, a funny old game,
With bouncing signals, they call us by name.
Through laughter and pranks, we form our great link,
In this web of connections, who's laughing? We think!

Round and round like a merry-go-round,
With twists and turns, you never know what's found.
A bracelet of buddies, forever in sync,
Eternal shenanigans, more fun than we think.

Each chuckle we share, a bond made of glue,
Stickier than honey, and just as fun too.
With every high-five and goofy old grin,
We're creating connections that never wear thin.

So let's toast to the circles of zany delight,
Where friendships are formed, and everything's bright.
In this grand network, where laughter's the key,
We're infinite players, just wild and free.

The Dance of Circles

Round we do sway, like leaves in the breeze,
In this dance of the circles, we twist with such ease.
With every odd step, we create quite a scene,
A comical ballet, where nothing is keen.

Gyrating with joy, we spin and we clap,
With pirouettes flailing, we fall in a flap.
But who cares for grace when you trip on your toes?
Laughter erupts as we tumble like prose!

The rhythm gets funky, the beat starts to thump,
We're not pros at this dance; we're merely a lump.
Yet joy fills the air, like confetti released,
In this circle of friends, we're all wildly pleased.

So grab me your buddy, let's twirl, let's prance,
In this merry-go-round of a comical dance.
With each silly move, let's loosen our souls,
The dance of the circles, the party unfolds!

Spirals of Love and Time

We spiral and twirl, adventures unplanned,
Like spaghetti we're winding, it's all quite unscanned.
With time on our side, we chuckle and spin,
In this loop of affection, everyone wins!

Our friendships are loops, like a rollercoaster ride,
With ups and downs, there's nowhere to hide.
In spirals of joy, we laugh 'til we cry,
Like a screwball comedy, we reach for the sky!

With every tight turn, we learn and we grow,
In the wildest of loops, we steal every show.
With hugs that are swirling, let's sip on a mime,
We're lost in the spirals, all reset by that time.

So follow the twists, let's make it our goal,
The journey is fun, and that's pretty droll.
In these spirals of laughter, we keep the good rhyme,
Forever entwined, we're just dancing through time!

Interlaced Journeys

Two souls met on a twisted road,
With ties so strong, they shared one load.
Their laughter echoed, like silly birds,
To bind their hearts without any words.

They tripped on love, fell into the fray,
With mismatched socks, they danced all day.
Wobbly steps on the path of delight,
Tangled paths, but oh what a sight!

They forged ahead, with giggles and glee,
As life threw curves, they'd just sip tea.
Their dreams interwove like a grand bouquet,
Who knew such fun could come out to play?

In their quirky dance, the world took a spin,
Finding joy in mess-ups, that's how they win.
Together they traveled, hand in hand,
Life's clumsy twirl—oh how grand!

Unbroken Circles

Life spins around like a hula hoop,
With wobbly grace, we all jump through.
Round and round with our friends by our side,
In laughter we fall, in love we abide.

A donut shaped bond, sweet and round,
We sprinkle on joy, it knows no bound.
With each silly game and odd little fight,
We circle each other, morning to night.

Every twist a new chance to embrace,
While juggling our joys, we trip at our pace.
From mismatched shoes to jokes about fate,
In our unbroken glam, we elevate.

Through ups and downs, we hold on tight,
Spinning through life, oh what a sight!
Our laughter a ring, shining so bright,
An endless loop of pure delight!

Intersection of Hearts

Two roads converged in a silly park,
Where hearts collide and laughter sparks.
With a wink and a smile, oh what a scene,
A jumble of bliss, love's sweet cuisine.

They brought their quirks, like mismatched shoes,
In the dance of love, you win or you lose.
But they chose to laugh, with their rhythm unique,
Bumping like cars in a comical streak.

Each intersection a chance to delight,
To weave their tales under warm moonlight.
With funnies and fumbles, they crafted a dance,
At every crossroad, they seized the chance.

So here's to the hearts adjusted and kind,
Who meet in the middle, all intertwined.
In the goofy chaos of life's crazy part,
They find their way, a humorous heart!

The Embrace of Cycles

In the merry-go-round of life's funny race,
We twist and we turn, as we pick up the pace.
With each dizzy spin and each silly quirk,
In cycles we laugh, it's all just a perk.

Round and round, our stories we share,
With a pinch of chaos, and not a care.
We fall off a swing, with giggles in tow,
In the embrace of cycles, our spirits grow.

Like rubber bands stretching with each heartfelt hug,
We're playful and free, in this wobbly tug.
Through loops and through turns, we weave and we ride,
A cycle of fun, with joy as our guide.

So spin me around on this whimsical spree,
In the embrace of cycles, just you and me.
With laughter as fuel and love as the core,
We'll roll through life, always wanting more!

Eternal Whispers of Connection

In a land where socks all roam,
Gloves unite to find a home.
Friendship sparks with every fling,
Who knew that laundry's such a thing?

Whispers shared while baking pie,
Sing to cupcakes, watch them fly.
Laughter echoes, hearts entwine,
Life's a dance, we feel divine.

Through every hug, a warmth we share,
Silly faces, just beware!
Together we create our lore,
In friendship's glow, we simply soar.

Let's skip and hop, the world's our stage,
Age doesn't matter, turn the page.
With every joke, connection grows,
In life's great play, who really knows?

Circles of Light and Love

Round and round, we twirl with glee,
Juggling dreams like a buzzing bee.
Frogs in hats, they dance and sing,
A merry-go-round of everything!

Candles flicker on a whim,
Silly faces, make hearts brim.
Join the conga, shuffle fast,
In circles of joy, we'll have a blast!

Balloons burst with laughter stored,
Chaos reigns, and we absorb.
Midnight snacks and stories tall,
With this crew, we have it all.

Shining bright like silly stars,
Life's a race, but don't run far.
Celebrate each quirky friend,
In circles where the fun won't end.

Embrace of Infinite Bonds

Hugs are sparked when pizza's near,
Slipping on cheese, we laugh and cheer.
Tango in the kitchen's glow,
A dance debacle? Steal the show!

Socks mismatched, a fashion crime,
Strutting proud, we waste no time.
Dancing wobbly, break the mold,
In silly arms, we feel so bold.

With jellybeans and joyful shouts,
Our voices join, we twist about.
From burger swaps to cupcake fights,
In friendship's glow, we reach new heights.

Waffles stacked, syrup cascades,
Chasing llamas through glade parades.
In goofy bonds, we find our tune,
Underneath the laughing moon.

Tokens of Togetherness

Gift-wrapped joy, what will we find?
Cookies baked, or socks combined?
Cards of laughter fill the space,
In every token, a smile's trace.

Cupcaps build a castle tall,
As we giggle and play ball.
Silly hats and toy raccoons,
Creating chaos 'neath the moon.

Every token tells our tale,
Of inside jokes, we cannot fail.
Friendship bracelets, proud we wear,
For every bond, we truly care.

Crayons drawn in colors bright,
Sketching laughter, pure delight.
Through every memory, love's the goal,
Together as one, we're always whole.

Mystical Emblems of Belonging

In a land where squirrels wear crowns,
The cats form bands, and dance around.
We all have symbols, ridiculous and bright,
A badge of our quirks, our laughter's delight.

Pick a hat, a sock, or maybe a shoe,
These tokens of friendship, oh so true.
Together we treasure these charms so silly,
In our odd little world, oh what a frilly!

We form a club of mismatched attire,
With wild tales spun that never tire.
Every twist and turn comes with a laugh,
In this circus of life, we find our path.

So here's to the charms that make us whole,
The whimsical tokens for every soul.
With giggles and quirks, we wear our pride,
In this funny brigade, side by side.

The Aura of Committed Souls

In a realm where muffins wear capes,
And coffee brews in funny shapes.
Love's commitment is a quirky tune,
Each day we dance beneath the moon.

We promise the laughter, the giggles, the fun,
Over pancakes stacked, we share a pun.
No solemn vows but cake on our face,
In this sweet love, there's endless grace.

We swap our dreams like trading cards,
Like children at play, we lower our guards.
With every mishap, we giggle and sigh,
A partnership rooted in the wittiest high!

So here's to the partners who make us whole,
With a laugh or two to soothe the soul.
May the fun never stop, let the chaos unfurl,
In this lively dance of our whimsical world.

Constellations of Intertwined Fates

Stars above with mischief in mind,
They doodle our paths, infinitely twined.
Each laugh a planet, each giggle a moon,
Our fates are a puzzle, a whimsical tune.

We gather in circles, like bottles of fizz,
With silly confessions that end with a whizz.
The universe winks at our chaotic flight,
As we tumble through life, gleefully bright.

With every laugh, we paint our own sky,
Mixing funny tales as time passes by.
We shine like constellations, pure joy in the mix,
In this cosmic jigsaw, the world's our fix.

So here's to the stars that guide us along,
In this stellar arena where silliness belongs.
With friends by our side, with every kind fate,
Together we orbit, oh what a great state!

Love's Unyielding Embrace

In meals filled with laughter, like pies on a plate,
We share all our stories, it's never too late.
Our love is a feast, with crumbs galore,
As we bumble through days, we find evermore.

With hugs that send giggles, and silly dance beats,
Our life is a parade with banquets of treats.
In every embrace, there's a snicker or pun,
This love that we cherish, oh how we run!

We twirl with delight like jubilant sprites,
Our hearts full of joy, a hundred spotlight nights.
In the arms of our laughter, we stubbornly stay,
Through mishaps and giggles, we'll find our way.

So here's to the love that keeps us in glee,
In the randomness of life, it's you and it's me.
With a wink and a nudge, embrace the oddball race,
For this fun-filled journey, it's our perfect place.

Echoes of Enduring Friendship

In a world where socks go missing,
And coffee's always spilling,
We laugh through every bickering,
Our joy a ring, ever thrilling.

We share odd snacks in the night,
And dance like no one is around,
With each silly joke, we ignite,
A bond that's laughter-bound.

Through awkward dates and flopped hairdos,
We cheer each other up so fast,
Like mismatched toys that somehow fuse,
Creating glee that's made to last.

So here's to us, the quirky crew,
Forever linked by crazy lore,
In this wacky circus we pursue,
Friendship's jest—our greatest score.

The Fabric of Interwoven Lives.

In the loom of laughter and delight,
Our stories twist and twirl, you see,
Like socks on laundry day—what a sight!
Together, weaving goofy glee.

We stitch up dreams with mismatched threads,
No pattern here, just wild intent,
With every chuckle, our colors spread,
In this messy quilt, we're all content.

Tangled tales from years gone by,
With every knot, a memory forms,
Like pasta dances at a feast—oh my!
Our lives a patchwork, full of warmth.

So grab your needles, let's create more,
Stitch by stitch, we'll laugh and grow,
In this fabric, love's at the core,
Together forever, this we know.

Emblems of Commitment

We pledge our socks to never stray,
And share the last slice of the pie,
In silly vows, we find our way,
Two peas in a pod, oh so spry!

Our promises are sweet and light,
With jellybeans and plans to dream,
In every giggle, love takes flight,
Committed, together we beam!

Each handshake's a pact, a friendly shout,
With cookies shared, we're bound so tight,
Through ups and downs, there's never doubt,
In this dance of ours, it feels so right.

So here's to us, our bonds so sweet,
In laughter's glow, we find our way,
With every mischief, our hearts compete,
Emblems of joy that will forever stay.

Circles of Light and Dark

In circles round, we spin and jest,
With shadows dancing in the sun,
Like little sprites that never rest,
We chase the laughter, oh so fun!

Through ups and downs, our secrets swirl,
In candlelight, the stories bloom,
We tease and twirl, a wild whirl,
Creating chaos in the room.

With silly hats and goofy wigs,
We celebrate in pure delight,
Together we dance, like jumping jigs,
In circles bright, we own the night.

So laugh with me, let worries part,
In this merry-go-round, we're whole,
With friendship's spark, we warm the heart,
In circles joined, each plays their role.

Emblems of Shared Journeys

In a world so vast and wild,
Two pals set off, laughter piled.
With mismatched socks and silly hats,
Finding joy in friendly spats.

Each step they take, a jest ensues,
Like wobbly penguins, they can't lose.
A map drawn in crayons, oh what a sight,
Their route to giggles, a pure delight.

From ice cream spills to running gags,
Through every challenge, no room for drags.
In every stumble, a dance is made,
Their shared journey a parade unafraid.

So here's to the bonds that make us grin,
With secret codes and silly spin.
Together they shine, the perfect duo,
In a circus of life, they steal the show!

Resonance of Kindred Spirits

Two hearts that beat in synchrony,
Like spoons that dance in a coffee spree.
With jokes that fly like shooting stars,
Their laughter echoes, no need for bars.

They share their dreams in goofy styles,
Wearing funny wigs, sharing smiles.
From baking fails to karaoke nights,
Kindred spirits reach new heights.

In cosmic realms of giggles galore,
They ride the waves of life's uproar.
With mismatched truths and playful lies,
Each moment together is a sweet surprise.

So let the world frown, they'll just beam,
For every day's a wacky dream.
In friendship's bond, they find their rule,
Together they sparkle, that's the fuel!

Vows in the Shape of Cycles

Round and round, they spin with glee,
In a dance that's wild and free.
With twirls that could make others dizzy,
They vow to keep it all quite fizzy.

Each loop they take a laugh behind,
Through ups and downs, love intertwined.
In circles drawn with chalky flair,
A promise made in silliness rare.

With hands unsteady, and hearts aglow,
Together they sway, putting on a show.
Like hula hoops of giggling delight,
Their vows shine bright, like stars at night.

So let them roll in circles wide,
With tickles and grins, they'll never hide.
In every twist, their spirits soar,
In love's embrace, forevermore!

Chalices of Heartfelt Exchange

Raise your cups, it's time to cheer,
With drinks of joy, let's draw near.
From bubbling soda to smoothies bright,
Each sip shared feels just right.

With silly straws and vibrant hues,
They swap their secrets, share their views.
A toast to moments, both big and small,
With shouts and doodles, they've got it all.

In every gulp, a giggle spills,
Like spontaneous dance in cozy thrills.
With clinks and cheers, they celebrate,
In heartfelt exchanges, they cultivate.

So pass the chalice, don't be shy,
With every sip, let laughter fly.
For in this toast, friendships grow,
In cups of joy, love's the flow!

Threads of Celestial Affection

In the sky, the stars do twirl,
While moonbeams tease the night's soft pearl.
A thread so fine, woven with glee,
Stitches hearts, you and me.

Laughter bubbles in cosmic delight,
As planets wobble, dancing in flight.
A little mischief in every glance,
We twirl and spin in this cosmic dance.

Galaxies giggle at our sweet fight,
Fingers tangled in the starlit night.
Cosmic yarns spun with vibrant hues,
Love's a quilt of delightful clues.

With each tick of the clock, we rise,
Lost in the laughter that never dies.
Stitched together by fingers of fate,
In this universe, we celebrate!

Unbroken Hoops of Destiny

Round and round the hoops do sway,
Destiny's path in a playful ballet.
Jumping through loop after loop,
Like a squirrel in a never-ending scoop.

Hurdles and rings in fields of jest,
Throwing our hats in a comical quest.
With every leap and twist we take,
We giggle at all the hoops we make.

Bouncing like kangaroos in the sun,
Life's silly games are just so fun!
Around and around, no end in sight,
We'll jump through hoops until the night.

With laughter echoing, we won't stop,
Like kids with candy, we just can't drop.
In circles of joy, we'll forever glide,
With our hearts wide open, side by side!

The Dance of Timeless Promises

We pirouette through promises bright,
With silly steps that feel just right.
Twists and turns on the floor of fate,
In our dance, let's celebrate!

Waltzing through the nights so clear,
Step on my foot, let's share a beer!
Giggles bubble as we lose our place,
A swirl of laughter, a comical chase.

In every spin, a promise made,
We kick up dust, our endless parade.
Two partners lost in a waltz so sweet,
With every misstep, our hearts skip a beat.

With every twirl, our joy expands,
In the dance of life, we take our stands.
Hand in hand, we'll shimmy and sway,
Making fun of life, come what may!

Infinity Encircled in Time

Time wraps us up in a giant bow,
Tick-tocking like a silly show.
Infinity spins in a mix-up flair,
As we giggle and lose, forgetting where.

Boundless loops in a race of glee,
Chasing the hours, you and me.
"What time is it?" we ask in jest,
"I've lost my socks, give me a rest!"

Circles of time with laughs in tow,
Round and around, where did it go?
In the crazy dance of life's grand scheme,
Together we float in a whimsical dream.

So let's cherish these moments sweet,
With laughter and joy, life is a treat.
Encircled in fun, forever we'll climb,
In this silly spiral, we're lost in time!

Bands of Affection

I lost my ring while munching a pie,
My finger felt naked, oh me, oh my!
But then I found it in a very strange place,
Right next to a squirrel, lunching with grace.

Now this little band has a story to tell,
Of pastries and critters who dance very well.
My ring may be silly, but it won't cause strife,
It's a tale of my love for both food and for life.

So every time I slip it back on,
I remember the laughs and the laughter we spawn.
Affection is quirky, a wild sort of jest,
And this ring of mine? It's simply the best!

Now every friend says "Please, let us see,
Your ring is as odd as a cup of cold tea!"
We giggle together, it's all in good fun,
In bands of affection, we're never outrun.

Unity in Eternity

Two halves of a joke, we laugh 'til we cry,
United like socks that all tend to fly.
Eternally fidgeting, we spin like balloons,
Love's a circus act, with swans and balloons.

My partner in chaos, my ring in disguise,
It's shiny and wild, with a hint of surprise.
When we put it on, it's an elastic embrace,
A bond that's forever, a slapstick in space.

We're like clowns in a rom-com, tumbling around,
With punches and pratfalls, and laughter abound.
You'll find us in corners, creating a scene,
Unity is messy, but it's joyful and keen!

So here's to our journeys in awkward delight,
Finding love in the mishaps and silly daylight.
With each clumsy step, let's dance on this track,
In unity's chaos, we never look back.

Duets of the Loop

In the great merry-go-round, we spin with a cheer,
Duets are our tunes, the laughter's sincere.
While I lose my shoe, my partner just grins,
Say, "Weren't those some moves? Let's do it again!"

Rings on our fingers, we twirl and we sway,
Like dizzy old puppies, we bark come what may.
Every slip, every trip, makes our love oh so bright,
We're rhymes in a comedy, dancing through night.

From twinkling confetti to jams we just make,
Sometimes it's chaos, like frosting on cake.
But who needs perfection? We're perfect in fun,
With loops and with giggles, we've already won!

So let's raise a toast to mishaps that bloom,
To laughter so loud, we could fill up a room.
In this quirky ballet, with moves that astound,
Our duets keep spinning, forever unbound.

Oaths in Motion

I promised myself I'd never trip twice,
Yet here comes my foot, and oh, what a slice!
Oaths that I make seem to slip through the cracks,
As my ring rolls away, and my dignity whacks.

In motion together, we swirl like a breeze,
Silly slip-ups bring an endless tease.
Love's not a straight road, it's a bumpy old ride,
With chars and with chuckles, there's nothing to hide.

So we vow to keep laughing, each tumbling fall,
Our oath ever-changing, we embrace it all.
With a wink and a nod, we sign with a grin,
Adventures await where the silliness begins!

So here's to our frolics and promises bright,
In joyful confusion, we'll dance through the night.
Oaths in motion, they shimmer and glide,
With laughter our compass, love's a fun ride!

www.ingramcontent.com/pod-product-compliance
Lightning Source LLC
Chambersburg PA
CBHW070002300426
43661CB00141B/143